PENGUIN BOOKS

SONGS OF THE GURUS

Khushwant Singh was India's best-known writer and columnist. He was founder-editor of *Yojana* and editor of the *Illustrated Weekly of India*, the *National Herald* and *Hindustan Times*. He is the author of classics such as *Train to Pakistan, I Shall Not Hear the Nightingale* (retitled as *The Lost Victory*) and *Delhi*. His latest novel, *The Sunset Club*, written when he was ninety-five, was published by Penguin Books in 2010. His non-fiction includes the classic two-volume *A History of the Sikhs*, a number of translations and works on Sikh religion and culture, Delhi, nature, current affairs and Urdu poetry. His autobiography, *Truth, Love and a Little Malice*, was published by Penguin Books in 2002.

Khushwant Singh was a member of Parliament from 1980 to 1986. He was awarded the Padma Bhushan in 1974 but returned the decoration in 1984 in protest against the storming of the Golden Temple in Amritsar by the Indian Army. In 2007, he was awarded the Padma Vibhushan. Among the other awards he has received are the Punjab Ratan, the Sulabh International award for the most honest Indian of the year, and honorary doctorates from several universities. He passed away in 2014 at the age of ninety-nine.

Arpana Caur was born in 1954 in Delhi. Her works have been exhibited since 1974 in India and abroad, and can be found in museums of modern art in Delhi, Mumbai, Bhopal, Chandigarh, Victoria and Albert Museum and Bradford in the UK, Singapore, Dusseldorf, Hiroshima, Los Angeles and San Francisco. She is inspired by her mother Ajeet Cour's writings, Gurbani, the Pahari miniature and Indian folk-art traditions. She has been a recipient of the Gold Medal in the sixth Triennele, apart from other awards and grants.

SONGS OF THE GURUS

KHUSHWANT SINGH

ILLUSTRATIONS BY ARPANA CAUR

RAVI
DAYAL

PENGUIN BOOKS

PENGUIN BOOKS

USA | Canada | UK | Ireland | Australia
New Zealand | India | South Africa | China

Penguin Books is part of the Penguin Random House group of companies
whose addresses can be found at global.penguinrandomhouse.com

Published by Penguin Random House India Pvt. Ltd
7th Floor, Infinity Tower C, DLF Cyber City,
Gurgaon 122 002, Haryana, India

First published in Viking by Penguin Books India in association with
Ravi Dayal Publisher 2008
Published in Penguin Books by Penguin Random House India and
Ravi Dayal Publisher 2016

10 9 8 7 6 5 4 3 2 1

ISBN 9780143427711

Typeset in Perpetua by Eleven Arts, New Delhi
Printed at Replika Press Pvt. Ltd, India

Contents

# Introduction

The Sikh religion, a synthesis of Hinduism and Islam, is among the youngest of the world's major religions. The word Sikh is derived from the Sanskrit 'shishya' or the Pali 'sikkha', meaning disciple. The Sikhs are the disciples of their ten Gurus and worship the Granth Sahib (or Adi Granth), which is a compilation of hymns composed by the Gurus and other saints of medieval India.

A striking feature of Sikhism is its emphasis on prayer. The form of the prayer is usually the repetition of the name of God and the chanting of hymns in God's praise. Most of these hymns are contained in the Granth Sahib, and the remaining few are to be found in the *Dasam Granth* of the tenth and last Guru, Gobind Singh. The hymns were composed by Hindu Bhaktas and Muslim Sufis—Farid, Namdev and Kabir, among others—and by the Gurus themselves, who were poets of great sensitivity. In this book I have put together a selection of hymns by the first five Gurus and the ninth and tenth Gurus (the sixth, seventh and eighth Gurus did not write any). Together, they communicate the essence of Sikhism.

The Sikh faith was founded by Nanak (1469–1539), the first Guru of the Sikhs. He was born in a village called Talwandi, about forty miles from Lahore. His parents were Hindus belonging to a Kshatriya subsect known as Bedis, that is, 'those who know the Vedas'. Nanak was taught a little Arabic and Persian, some Sanskrit, Hindi and accounting. But his mind was never in his work. He spent his time meditating and seeking the company of wandering hermits. His parents found a wife for him when he was eighteen, and the couple had two sons. But Nanak soon lost interest in his family and reverted to meditating and wandering. A Muslim rebeck-player, Mardana, joined him, becoming his first disciple. Nanak composed hymns, Mardana set them to music, and the two began to organize community hymn-singing.

In the year 1499, when Nanak was thirty years old, he had a mystic experience. One morning while bathing in a stream, he disappeared under the water. According to his biographers, he found himself in the presence of God who spoke to him thus:

'Nanak, I am with thee. Through thee will my Name be magnified. Go into the world to pray and teach mankind how to pray. But be not sullied by the ways of the world. Let your life be one of praise of the Word (Nam), and of charity (daan), ablution (ishnaan), service (seva) and prayer (simran).'

Nanak was missing for three days and nights. When he came back, the first thing he said to the people who thronged to greet him was, 'There is no Hindu; there is no Mussalman.'

Nanak took to preaching. Accompanied by Mardana, he travelled extensively, within India and also abroad (it is believed that he travelled to places as distant as Sri Lanka, Tibet and Mecca). He visited many holy cities of the Hindus and the Muslims, pointing out the folly of meaningless ritual and emphasizing the common aspects of the two faiths. He spent his last years in a town called Kartarpur—meaning 'The abode of the Creator'— preaching and composing and singing hymns. He died in 1539 at the age of seventy. He was acclaimed by both Hindus and Muslims as the king of holy men.

Nanak's teaching reveals the influence of both Hinduism and Islam. By the fifteenth century these religious systems had evolved some beliefs that had much in common. It was from the teachings of the Muslim Sufis, notably Sheikh Farid, and the Bhaktas, primarily Kabir, that Nanak drew his inspiration. From Islam, Nanak took its unqualified monotheism, rejection of idolatry and of the caste system. From Hinduism, he borrowed the metaphysics of the Upanishads and the Gita.

He elevated reality (sat) to the position of the One Supreme God. He accepted the theory of karma and transmigration of souls. The path he advocated was of bhakti, emphasizing the worship of the name of God (Nam-marga). He rejected asceticism and propagated the grihastha-dharma (religion for the householder) and advocated the necessity of taking on a guru and keeping company with holy men (saadh sangat). Nanak also set great store by community hymn-singing (kirtan). He advised his followers to rise before dawn and listen to religious music, for he believed that in the stillness of the ambrosial hours (amritvela), one is best able to commune with God.

When Nanak died he left behind him a small community of Hindus and Muslims who described themselves as Nanak-panthis—followers of Nanak's way. They could at best be described as a group dissenting from both Hinduism and Islam. It was left to Nanak's successors to mould this group into a community with its own language and literature, religious beliefs and institutions, traditions and conventions.

The second Guru, Angad (1504–52), was a disciple of Guru Nanak and was chosen by Nanak as his successor in preference to his own sons. The third Guru, Amar Das (1479–1574), was, in similar fashion, chosen from among Angad's disciples. Guru Angad developed the Gurmukhi script by combining the scripts current in northern India at the time. He then collected the writings of Nanak and added some of his own to the compilation. Angad also established centres (manjis) for the propagation of Nanak's teachings. These manjis became meeting places for Sikhs, and later on temples (gurdwaras) sprang up in their place. Amar Das consolidated Angad's work by increasing the number of manjis and introducing innovations to give Sikhism an identity distinct from Brahminical Hinduism. He preached against the seclusion of women, advocated monogamy, encouraged inter-caste alliances and forbade sati.

The fourth Guru, Ram Das (1534–81), laid the foundation of the temple at Amritsar. This gurdwara—famous today as Harmandir Sahib or the Golden Temple—was elevated to the status of the holiest of Sikh shrines by his successor, Arjan (1563–1606), who also took definite steps towards organizing the Sikh community. What Angad had started, Arjan completed. He, along with his chief disciple Gurdas (1559–1637), continued the compilation started by the second Guru, and incorporated in it the writings of Hindu and Muslim saints. This became the Adi Granth or Granth Sahib, the holy scripture of the Sikhs. He was also responsible for the construction of temples at Taran Taran, Amritsar and Kartarpur, which became places of pilgrimage.

Guru Arjan's organizing activities attracted the notice of the Mughal officials in Punjab; they began to see the new faith as a political threat, and things inevitably went out of control. Arjan was arrested and, after considerable torture, executed at Lahore. He became the first and perhaps the most important martyr in Sikh history.

After the death of Guru Arjan, Sikhism went through a transformation. It is said that the last message Arjan sent for his son and successor was: 'Let him sit fully armed on his throne and maintain an army to the best of his ability.' Hargobind (1606–45) accepted his father's advice and decided to train his followers in the art of defence. He girded himself with two swords, one signifying the spiritual and the other temporal leadership. By the time of his death, the Sikhs had already become a significant fighting force in the hill tracts and won several engagements against Hindu chieftains and local Muslim militia.

Guru Hargobind was followed by his grandson Har Rai (1630–61), a man of peace who adhered strictly to the routine of prayer and selfless service exhorted by Nanak. Upon his death, his youngest son, Hari Krishen (1656–64), was proclaimed Guru at the age of five, but he died of smallpox barely three years later.

The final transformation of the Sikhs into a militant sect came with the last of the ten Gurus, Gobind Singh. In the autumn of 1675, Gobind's father, the ninth Guru, Tegh Bahadur (1621–75), was summoned to Delhi by the Mughal Emperor Aurangzeb and ordered to accept conversion to Islam. The legend goes that he refused and volunteered to perform a miracle whereby the executioner's sword would fail to sever his head from his body. He wrote some words on a piece of paper and tied it round his neck with a thread like a charm. When he was decapitated the message on the paper was seen to read: '*Sirr diya, pur sirrar na diya*'—'I gave my head but not my faith'. It is also said that shortly before he was executed Tegh Bahadur had repeated Arjan's advice to his son about arming the Sikhs.

Guru Gobind (1666–1708) assumed the leadership of the Sikh community when he was only ten years of age. He spent the first few years studying Persian, Sanskrit and the Hindu scriptures, and preparing himself for his mission. He realized that if his followers were to be saved from extinction, they had not only to be taught the use of arms but also convinced of the morality of the use of force. 'When all other means have failed, it is righteous to draw the sword,' he said. Even the conception of God became a militant one: He was timeless as death; His symbol was steel. Armed with these mental concepts, Gobind Singh set about 'training the sparrow to hunt the hawk and one man to fight a legion'.

On the Hindu New Year's Day in 1699, Gobind assembled his followers and initiated five of them, whom he called his Punj Piyaras (the Five Beloved), into a new fraternity which he named the Khalsa, or 'the pure'. Of these five, one was a Kshatriya and the other four belonged to the lower castes. They were made to drink Amrit (consecrated water) out of the same bowl and given new names with the suffix 'Singh' (lion). They swore to observe the 'Five K's', namely, to wear their hair and beard unshorn (kesh); to carry a comb in the hair (kangha); to wear a pair of shorts (kuchha); to wear a steel bangle on the right wrist (kara); and to carry a dagger at the waist (kirpan). Gobind further bade the initiates rid themselves of their family ties, their professions, their creed and ritual, and have no loyalties except to the Khalsa. After baptising the five, he had himself baptised by them. At the end of the ceremony, the Guru hailed his Punj Piyaras with a new greeting—'*Wah guru ji ka khalsa, Wah guru ji ki Fateh*': 'The Khalsa are the chosen of God, Victory be to our God.'

A significant step Gobind Singh took was to declare the line of Gurus at an end after him. He did this while all his four sons were alive. He divided the concept of Guruship into three—personal, religious and temporal. The first he said would end with him. The second would subsist for ever in the scriptures, and the Granth Sahib was henceforth to be regarded as the symbolic representation of the ten Gurus. Temporal leadership he vested in the community, so that all decisions taken by the majority of a representative assembly became binding on the rest as if it were the order of the Guru himself (gurumat).

The Sikhs believe in the unity of God and equate God with truth. Although Sikh monotheism has an abstract quality, there is nothing vague about it. The preamble to the morning prayer, Japji, which is recited as an introduction to all religious ceremonies and is known as the Mool Mantra, the basic belief, states:

> There is One God.
> He is the supreme truth.
> He, the Creator,
> Is without fear and without hate.
> He, the Omnipresent,
> Pervades the universe.
> He is not born,
> Nor does He die to be born again.
> (Nanak)

There was a change of emphasis in the conception of God in the writing of the tenth Guru. To him, although God was still One, and the Creator, the aspect of timelessness and the power to destroy was more important. Gobind Singh described God as Akal Purukh (The Timeless One):

Time is the only God,
The primal and the final,
The creator and the destroyer.
How can words describe Him?

The attitudes of the two Gurus which seem at first sight to be divergent are not really so. The basic factors in the conception of God were oneness and truth. Other attributes, such as omnipresence, omniscience, formlessness, timelessness, and the power to destroy evil, were complementary. Guru Gobind Singh only gave them prominence by constant emphasis. Although God is without form (nirankar) or substance and is beyond human comprehension, by righteous living one can invoke His grace. In the first verse of the morning prayer, Nanak himself said:

Not by thought alone
Can He be known,
Though one think a hundred thousand times . . .
How then shall Truth be known?
How the veil of false illusion torn?
O Nanak, thus runneth the writ divine:
The righteous path—let it be thine.

The Sikh emphasis on action as a means to salvation is a departure from the predestination, and consequent passiveness, of Hindu belief. Nanak, who was fond of using rural similes, wrote:

As a team of oxen are we driven
By the ploughman, our Teacher.
By the furrows made are thus writ
Our actions—on the earth, our paper.
The sweat of labour is as beads

Falling, by the ploughman as seeds sown:
We reap according to our measure,
Some for ourselves to keep, some to others give.
O Nanak, this is the way to truly live.

Although Sikhism accepts the Hindu theory of karma and life hereafter, it speaks of the possibility of rising above the maze in which life, death and rebirth go on, independent, as it were, of human volition. The Sikh religion states categorically that the first form given to life is the human ('Thou has the body of man, now is thy turn to meet God'—Arjan). Human actions then determine the subsequent forms of life to be assumed after death. It thus advocates that by righteous living and grace it is possible to escape the vicious circle of life and death and attain salvation.

The Sikh religion, believing as it does in the unity and formlessness of God, expressly forbids the worship of idols and emblems. Guru Nanak, while attending the evening service at a Hindu temple where a salver full of small oil lamps and incense was being waved in front of the idol, composed this verse:

The firmament is Thy salver,
The sun and moon Thy lamps,
The galaxy of stars
As pearls scattered.
The woods of sandal are Thine incense,
The forests Thy flowers,
But what worship is this
O Destroyer of Fear?

God being an abstraction, godliness is conceived as an attribute. The way of acquiring godliness or salvation is to obey the will of God. The means of ascertaining God's will are, as in other theological systems, unspecified and subject to human speculation. They are largely rules of moral conduct which are the basis of human society. Sikhism advocates association with

men of religion for guidance. Hence the importance of the guru or the teacher and the institution of discipleship.

The Sikhs do not worship human beings as incarnations of God. The Sikh Gurus themselves insisted that they were human like other human beings and were on no account to be worshipped. Guru Nanak constantly referred to himself as the slave and servant of God. Guru Gobind Singh, who was the author of most of the Sikh practice and ritual, was conscious of the danger of having divinity imposed on him by his followers. He explained his mission in life:

> For though my thoughts were lost in prayer
> At the feet of Almighty God,
> I was ordained to establish a sect and lay down its rules.
> But whosoever regards me as Lord
> Shall be damned and destroyed.
>
> I am—and of this let there be no doubt—
> I am but the slave of God, as other men are,
> A beholder of the wonders of creation.

Godliness being the aim of human endeavour, the lives and teachings of the Gurus are looked upon as aids towards its attainment. 'On meeting a true Guru,' said Nanak, 'doubt is dispelled and wanderings of the mind restrained.'

The compositions of the Gurus were always considered sacred by their followers. Guru Nanak said that in his hymns 'the True Guru manifested Himself, because they were composed at His orders and heard by Him'. The fourth Guru, Ram Das, said: 'Look upon the words of the true Guru as the supreme truth, for God and the Creator hath made him utter the words.' When Arjan formally installed the Granth Sahib in the Harmandir Sahib at

Amritsar, he ordered his followers to treat it with the same reverence they accorded their Gurus. By the time of Guru Gobind Singh, copies of the Granth had been installed in most gurdwaras. Quite naturally, when he declared the line of succession of Gurus ended, he asked his followers to turn to the Granth for guidance and look upon it as the symbolic representation of the ten Gurus. (His own *Dasam Granth* is read with reverence but does not form part of Sikh rituals, except at the ceremony of baptism.)

The Granth Sahib contains the writings of the first five Gurus, the ninth Guru, and a couplet by Guru Gobind Singh. A large part of the book consists of the writings of Hindu and Muslim saints of the time, chiefly those of Kabir, who, like Nanak, was claimed by both Hindus and Muslims as their saint. The compositions of the bards who accompanied the different Gurus are also incorporated in the Granth.

The language used by the Sikh Gurus was Punjabi of the fifteenth and sixteenth centuries. Other writings are in old Hindi, Persian, Sanskrit, Gujarati, Marathi and other dialects of northern India. The entire work is set to measures of classical Indian music. The hymns are not arranged by author or subject matter but divided into thirty-one ragas in which they are meant to be sung.

The Granth Sahib is the central object of Sikh worship and ritual. In all gurdwaras, copies of the Granth are placed under a canopy. The book itself is draped in cloth, usually richly embroidered. It is opened with prayer and ceremonial each morning and similarly closed in the evening. Worshippers appear before it barefooted and with their heads covered. They make obeisance before it, and offerings of money or food are placed on the cloth draping the book. Akhand Path, the ceremony of non-stop reading of the Granth Sahib by relays of worshippers, takes two days and nights and is performed on important religious festivals and private functions. Sikh children are named by being given a name beginning with the first letter appearing on the page at which the Granth may open. Sikh youths are baptised with recitation of prayers in front of the Granth. Sikh couples are married to the singing of hymns from the Granth, while they walk round it four times. On death, hymns are read aloud in the dying person's ear, and on cremation, they are chanted as the flames consume the body.

Despite all this, the Granth Sahib is not like an idol in a Hindu temple or a crucifix in a church. It is the source and not the object of prayer or worship. The Sikhs revere it because it contains the teachings of their Gurus. It is more a book of divine wisdom than the word of God. Its songs show the path that leads to the True One.

GURU
NANAK
{1469–1539}

There are 974 hymns by Guru Nanak in the Adi Granth.

*J*apji

THE MORNING PRAYER

(When he compiled the Adi Granth or Granth Sahib, the fifth Guru, Arjan Dev, gave Japji the first place in the sacred anthology. It remains the most important prayer of the Sikhs.)

There is One God.
He is the supreme truth.
He, the Creator,
Is without fear and without hate.
He, the Omnipresent,
Pervades the universe.
He is not born,
Nor does He die to be born again.
By His grace shalt thou worship Him.

Before time itself
There was truth.
When time began to run its course
He was the truth.
Even now, He is the truth
And evermore shall truth prevail.

1

Not by thought alone
Can He be known,
Though one think
A hundred thousand times;
Not in solemn silence
Nor in deep meditation.
Though fasting yields an abundance of virtue
It cannot appease the hunger for truth.
No, by none of these,
Nor by a hundred thousand other devices,
Can God be reached.
How then shall the Truth be known?
How the veil of false illusion torn?
O Nanak, thus runneth the writ divine,
The righteous path—let it be thine.

2

By Him are all forms created,
By Him infused with life and blessed,
By Him are some to excellence elated,
Others born lowly and depressed.
By His writ some have pleasure, others pain;
By His grace some are saved,
Others doomed to die, relive, and die again.
His will encompasseth all, there be none beside.
O Nanak, he who knows, hath no ego and no pride.

3

Who has the power to praise His might?
Who has the measure of His bounty?
Of His portents who has the sight?
Who can value His virtue, His deeds, His charity?
Who has the knowledge of His wisdom,
Of His deep, impenetrable thought?

How worship Him who creates life,
Then destroys,
And having destroyed doth recreate?
How worship Him who appeareth far
Yet is ever present and proximate?

There is no end to His description,
Though the speakers and their speeches be legion.

He the Giver ever giveth,
We who receive grow weary,
On His bounty humanity liveth
From primal age to posterity.

4

God is the Master, God is Truth,
His name spelleth love divine,
His Creatures ever cry: 'O give, O give,'
He the bounteous doth never decline.
What then in offering shall we bring
That we may see His court above?
What then shall we say in speech
That hearing may evoke His love?

In the ambrosial hours of fragrant dawn
On truth and greatness ponder in meditation,
Though action determine how thou be born,
Through grace alone cometh salvation.

O Nanak, this need we know alone,
That God and Truth are two in one.

5

He cannot be proved, for He is uncreated;
He is without matter, self-existent.
They that serve shall honoured be,
O Nanak, the Lord is most excellent.

Praise the Lord, hear them that do Him praise,
In your hearts His name be graven,
Sorrows from your soul erase
And make your hearts a joyous haven.

The Guru's word has the sage's wisdom,
The Guru's word is full of learning,
For though it be the Guru's word
God Himself speaks therein.

Thus run the words of the Guru:
'God is the destroyer, preserver and creator,
God is the Goddess too.
Words to describe are hard to find,
I would venture if I knew.'
This alone my teacher taught,
There is but one Lord of all creation,
Forget Him not.

6

If it please the Lord
In holy waters would I bathe,
If it pleases Him not,
Worthless is that pilgrimage.

This is the law of all creation,
That nothing's gained save by action.
Thy mind, wherein buried lie
Precious stones, jewels, gems,
Shall opened be if thou but try
And hearken to the Guru's word.

This the Guru my teacher taught,
There is but one Lord of all creation,
Forget Him not.

7

Were life's span extended to the four ages
And ten times more,
Were one known over the nine continents
Ever in humanity's fore,
Were one to achieve greatness
With a name noised over the earth,
If one found not favour with the Lord
What would it all be worth?
Among the worms be as vermin,
By sinners be accused of sin.

O Nanak, the Lord fills the vicious with virtue,
The virtuous maketh more true.
Knowest thou of any other
Who in turn could the Lord thus favour?

8

By hearing the word
    Men achieve wisdom, saintliness, courage, and
        contentment.

By hearing the word
    Men learn of the earth, the power that
        supports it, and the firmament.

By hearing the word
    Men learn of the upper and nether
        regions, of islands and continents.

By hearing the word
    Men conquer fear of death and the elements.

O Nanak, the word hath such magic for the worshippers,
    Those that hear, death do not fear,
    Their sorrows end and sins disappear.

9

By hearing the word
    Mortals are to godliness raised.
By hearing the word
    The foul-mouthed are filled with pious praise.

By hearing the word
    Are revealed the secrets of the body and of nature.
By hearing the word
    Is acquired the wisdom of all the scriptures.

O Nanak, the word hath such magic for the worshippers,
    Those that hear, death do not fear,
    Their sorrows end and sins disappear.

10

By hearing the word
    One learns of truth, contentment, and is wise.
By hearing the word
    The need for pilgrimages does not arise.
By hearing the word
    The student achieves scholastic distinction.
By hearing the word
    The mind is easily led to meditation.

O Nanak, the word hath such magic for the worshippers,
    Those that hear, death do not fear,
    Their sorrows end and sins disappear.

11

By hearing the word
    One sounds the depths of virtue's sea.
By hearing the word
    One acquires learning, holiness, and royalty.
By hearing the word
    The blind see and their paths are visible.

By hearing the word
    The fathomless becomes fordable.

O Nanak, the word hath such magic for the worshippers,
    Those that hear, death do not fear,
    Their sorrows end and sins disappear.

12

The believer's bliss one cannot describe,
He who endeavours regrets in the end,
There is no paper, pen, nor any scribe
Who can the believer's state comprehend.

The name of the Lord is immaculate.
He who would know must have faith.

13

The believer hath wisdom and understanding;
The believer hath knowledge of all the spheres;
The believer shall not stumble in ignorance,
Nor of death have any fears.

The name of the Lord is immaculate,
He who would know must have faith.

14

The believer's way is of obstructions free;
The believer is honoured in the presence sublime;

The believer's path is not lost in futility,
For faith hath taught him law divine.

The name of the Lord is immaculate,
He who would know must have faith.

15

The believer reaches the gate of salvation;
His kith and kin he also saves.
The believer beckons the congregation,
Their souls are saved from transmigration.

The name of the Lord is immaculate,
He who would know must have faith.

16

Thus are chosen the leaders of men,
Thus honoured in God's estimation;
Though they grace the courts of kings,
Their minds are fixed in holy meditation.
Their words are weighed with reason,
They know that God's works are legion.

Law which like the fabled bull supports the earth
Is of compassion born;
Though it bind the world in harmony,
Its strands are thin and worn.
He who the truth would learn
Must know of the bull and the load it bore,

For there are worlds besides our own
And beyond them many more.
Who is it that bears these burdens?
What power bears him that beareth them?

Of creatures of diverse kinds and colours
The ever-flowing pen hath made record.
Can anyone write what it hath writ
Or say how great a task was it?
How describe His beauty and His might?
His bounty how estimate?
How speak of Him who with one word
Did the whole universe create,
And made a thousand rivers flow therein?

What might have I to praise Thy might?
I have not power to give it praise.
Whatever be Thy wish, I say Amen.
Mayst Thou endure, O Formless One.

17

There is no count of those who pray,
Nor of those who Thee adore;
There is no count of those who worship,
Nor of those who by penance set store.
There is no count of those who read the holy books aloud
Nor of those who think of the world's sorrows and lament.
There is no count of sages immersed in thought and reason,
Nor of those who love humanity and are benevolent.
There is no count of warriors who match their strength with steel,
Nor of those who contemplate in peace and are silent.

What might have I to praise Thy might?
I have not power to give it praise.
Whatever be Thy wish, I say Amen.
Mayst Thou endure, O Formless One.

18

There is no count of fools who will not see,
Nor of thieves who live by fraud,
There is no count of despots practising tyranny,
Nor of those whose hands are soiled with blood.
There is no count of those who sin and go free,
Nor of liars caught in the web of falsehood,
There is no count of the polluted who live on filth,
Nor of the evil-tongued weighed down with calumny.
Of such degradation, O Nanak, also think.

What might have I to praise Thy might?
I have not power to give it praise.
Whatever be Thy wish, I say Amen.
Mayst Thou endure, O Formless One.

19

Though there is no count of Thy names and habitations,
Nor of Thy regions uncomprehended,
Yet many there have been with reason perverted
Who to Thy knowledge have pretended.
Though by words alone we give Thee name and praise,
And by words, reason, worship, and Thy virtue compute;
Though by words alone we write and speak

And by words our ties with Thee constitute;
The word does not its Creator bind,
What Thou ordainest we receive,
Thy creations magnify Thee,
Thy name in all places find.

What might have I to praise Thy might?
I have not power to give it praise.
Whatever be Thy wish, I say Amen.
Mayst Thou endure, O Formless One.

20

As hands or feet besmirched with slime,
Water washes white;
As garments dark with grime
Rinsed with soap are made light;
So when sin soils the soul
Prayer alone shall make it whole.

Words do not the saint or sinner make,
Action alone is written in the book of fate,
What we sow that alone we take;
O Nanak, be saved or forever transmigrate.

21

Pilgrimage, austerity, mercy, almsgiving, and charity
Bring merit, be it as little as the mustard seed;
But he who hears, believes, and cherishes the word,
An inner pilgrimage and cleansing is his meed.

All virtue is Thine, for I have none,
Virtue follows a good act done.
Blessed Thou the Creator, the Prayer, the Primal
Truth and beauty and longing eternal.
What was the time, what day of the week,
What the month, what season of the year,
When Thou didst create the earthly sphere?
The Pandit knows it not, nor is it writ in his Puran;
The Qadi knows it not, though he reads and copies the Koran.
The Yogi knows not the date nor the day of the week,
He knows not the month or even the season.
Only Thou who made it all can speak,
For knowledge is Thine alone.

How then shall I know Thee, how describe, praise, and name?
O Nanak, many there be who pretend to know, each bolder in his claim.
All I say is: 'Great is the Lord, great His name;
What He ordains comes to be,'
O Nanak, he who sayeth more shall hereafter regret his stupidity.

22

Numerous worlds there be in regions beyond the skies and below,
But the research-weary scholars say, we do not know.
The Hindu and the Muslim books are full of theories; the answer is but one.
If it could be writ, it would have been, but the writer thereof be none.
O Nanak, say but this, the Lord is great, in His knowledge He is alone.

23

Worshippers who praise the Lord know not His greatness,
As rivers and rivulets that flow into the sea know not its vastness.

Mighty kings with domains vaster than the ocean,
With wealth piled high in a mountainous heap
Are less than the little ant
That the Lord's name in its heart doth keep.

24

Infinite His goodness, and the ways of exaltation;
Infinite His creation and His benefaction;
Infinite the sights and sounds, infinite His great design;
Infinite its execution, infinite without confine.
Many there be that cried in pain to seek the end of all ending,
Their cries were all in vain, for the end is past understanding.
It is the end of which no one knoweth,
The more one says the more it groweth.
The Lord is of great eminence, exalted is His name.
He who would know His height, must in stature be the same.

He alone can His own greatness measure.
O Nanak, what He gives we must treasure.

25

Of His bounty one cannot write too much,
He the great Giver desires not even a mustard seed;
Even the mighty beg at His door, and others such
Whose numbers can never be conceived.
There be those who receive but are self-indulgent,
Others who get but have no gratitude.
There be the foolish whose bellies are never filled,
Others whom hunger's pain doth ever torment.
All this comes to pass as Thou hast willed.

Thy will alone breaks mortal bonds,
No one else hath influence.
The fool who argues otherwise
Shall be smitten into silence.
The Lord knows our needs, and gives,
Few there be that count their blessings,
He who is granted gratitude and power to praise,
O Nanak, is the king of kings.

26

His goodness cannot be priced or traded,
Nor His worshippers valued, nor their store;
Priceless too are dealers in the market sacred
With love and peace evermore.
Perfect His law and administration,
Precise His weights and measures;
Boundless His bounty and His omens,
Infinite mercy in His orders.
How priceless Thou art one cannot state,
Those who spoke are mute in adoration,
The readers of the scriptures expatiate,
Having read, are lost in learned conversation.
The great gods Brahma and Indra do Thee proclaim,
So do Krishna and his maidens fair;
Siva and the Saivites do Thee name.
The Buddhas Thou made, Thy name bear.
The demons and the demigods,
Men, brave men, seers, and the sainted,
Having discoursed and discussed
Have spoken and departed.

If Thou didst many more create
Not one could any more state,
For Thou art as great as is Thy pleasure.
O Nanak, Thou alone knowest Thy measure.
He who claims to know blasphemeth
And is the worst among the stupidest.

27

Sodar—(Te Deum)

Where is the gate, where the mansion,
From whence Thou watchest all creation,
Where sounds of musical melodies,
Of instruments playing, minstrels singing,
Are joined in divine harmony?
There the breezes blow, the waters run and the fires burn,
There Dharamraj, the King of death, sits in state;
There the recording angels Chitra and Gupta write
For Dharamraj to read and adjudicate.
There are the gods Isvara and Brahma,
The goddess Devi of divine grace;
There Indra sits on his celestial throne
And lesser gods, each in his place.
There ascetics in deep meditation,
Holy men in contemplation,
The pure of heart, the continent,
Men of peace and contentment,
Doughty warriors never yielding,
Thy praises are ever singing.
From age to age, the pandit and the sage
Do Thee exalt in their study and their writing.

There maidens fair, heart bewitching,
Who inhabit the earth, the upper and the lower regions,
Thy praises chant in their singing.
By the gems that Thou didst create,
In the sixty-eight places of pilgrimage,
Is Thy name exalted.
By warriors strong and brave in strife,
By the sources four from whence came life,
Of egg or womb, of sweet or seed,
Is Thy name magnified.
The regions of the earth, the heavens and the universe
That Thou didst make and dost sustain,
Sing to Thee and praise Thy name.
Only those Thou lovest and with whom Thou art pleased
Can give Thee praise and in Thy love be steeped.
Others too there must be who Thee acclaim,
I have no memory of knowing them
Nor of knowledge, O Nanak, make a claim.
He alone is the Master True, Lord of the word, ever the same,
He Who made creation is, shall be and shall ever remain;
He Who made things of diverse species, shapes, and hues,
Beholds that His handiwork His greatness proves.
What He wills He ordains,
To Him no one can an order give,
For He, O Nanak, is the King of Kings,
As He wills so we must live.

28

As a beggar goes a-begging,
Bowl in one hand, staff in the other,

Rings in his ears, in ashes smothered,
So go thou forth in life.
With ear-rings made of contentment,
With modesty thy begging bowl,
Meditation the fabric of thy garment,
Knowledge of death thy cowl,
Let thy mind be chaste, virginal clean,
Faith the staff on which to lean.
Thou shalt then thy fancy humiliate,
With mind subdued, the world subjugate.

Hail! And to Thee be salutation.
Thou art primal, Thou art pure,
Without beginning, without termination,
In single form, forever endure.

29

From the storehouse of compassion
Seek knowledge for thy food.
Let thy heartbeat be the call of the conch shell
Blown in gratitude.

He is the Lord, His is the will, His the creation,
He is the Master of destiny, of union and separation.

Hail! And to Thee be salutation.
Thou art primal, Thou art pure,
Without beginning, without termination,
In single form, forever endure.

30

Maya, mythical goddess in wedlock divine,
Bore three gods accepted by all,
The creator of the world, the one who preserves,
And the one who adjudges its fall.
But it is God alone Whose will prevails
Others but their obedience render.
He sees and directs, but is by them unseen,
That of all is the greatest wonder.

Hail! And to Thee be salutation.
Thou art primal, Thou art pure,
Without beginning, without termination,
In single form, forever endure.

31

He hath His prayer-mat in every region,
In every realm His store.
To human beings He doth apportion
Their share for once and evermore.
The Maker having made doth His own creation view.
O Nanak, He made truth itself, for He Himself is true.

Hail! And to Thee be salutation.
Thou art primal, Thou art pure,
Without beginning, without termination,
In single form, forever endure.

32

Were I given a hundred thousand tongues instead of one
And the hundred thousand multiplied twenty-fold,
A hundred thousand times would I say, and say again,
The Lord of all the worlds is One.
That is the path that leads
These the steps that mount,
Ascend thus to the Lord's mansion
And with Him be joined in unison.
The sound of the songs of Heaven thrills
The like of us who crawl, but desire to fly.
O Nanak, His grace alone it is that fulfils,
The rest mere prattle, and a lie.

33

Ye have no power to speak or in silence listen,
To grant or give away.
Ye have no power to live or die.
Ye have no power to acquire wealth and dominion,
To compel the mind to thought or reason,
To escape the world and fly.

He who hath the pride of power, let him try and see.
O Nanak, before the Lord there is no low or high degree.

34

He Who made the night and day,
The days of the week and the seasons,
He Who made the breezes blow, the waters run

The fires and the lower regions,
Made the earth—the temple of Law.

He Who made creatures of diverse kinds
With a multitude of names,
Made this the Law—
By thought and deed be judged forsooth,
For God is true and dispenseth truth.
There the elect His court adorn,
And God Himself their actions honours;
There are sorted deeds that were done and bore fruit
From those that to action could never ripen.
This, O Nanak, shall hereafter happen.

35

In the realm of justice there is law;
In the realm of knowledge there is reason.
Wherefore are the breezes, the waters and fire,
Gods that preserve and destroy, Krishnas and Sivas?
Wherefore are created forms, colours, attire,
Gods that create, the many Brahmas?

Here one strives to comprehend
The golden mount of knowledge ascend,
And learn as did the sage Dhruva.

Wherefore are the thunders and lightning,
The moons and suns,
The world and its regions?
Wherefore are the sages, seers, wise men,
Goddesses, false prophets, demons and demigods,
Wherefore are there jewels in the ocean?

How many forms of life there be,
How many tongues,
How many kings of proud ancestry?

Of these things many strive to know,
Many the slaves of reason.
Many there are, O Nanak, their numbers are legion.

36

As in the realm of knowledge reason is triumphant,
And yields a myriad joys,
So in the realm of bliss is beauty resplendent.
There are fashioned forms of great loveliness;
Of them it is best to remain silent
Than hazard guesses and then repent.
There too are fashioned consciousness, understanding, mind, and reason,
The genius of the sage and seer, the power of men superhuman.

37

In the realm of action, effort is supreme,
Nothing else prevails.
There dwell doughty warriors brave and strong,
With hearts full of godliness,
And celestial maidens of great loveliness
Who sing their praise.
They cannot die nor be beguiled
For God Himself in their hearts resides.
There too are congregations of holy men
Who rejoice, for the Lord in their midst presides.

In the realm of truth is the Formless One
Who, having created, watches His creation

And graces us with the blessed vision.
There are the lands, the earths and the spheres
Of whose description there is no limit;
There by a myriad forms are a myriad purposes fulfilled,
What He ordains is in them instilled.
What He beholds, thinks and contemplates,
O Nanak, is too hard to state.

38

If thou must make a gold coin true
Let thy mint these rules pursue.
In the forge of continence
Let the goldsmith be a man of patience,
His tools be made of knowledge,
His anvil made of reason;
With the fear of God the bellows blow,
With prayer and austerity make the fire glow,
Pour the liquid in the mould of love,
Print the name of the Lord thereon,
And cool it in the holy waters.
For thus in the mint of Truth the word is coined,
Thus those who are graced are to work enjoined.
O Nanak, by His blessing have joy everlasting.

Slok (Epilogue)

Air, water, and earth,
Of these are we made.
Air like the Guru's word gives the breath of life
To the babe born to the great mother earth
Sired by the waters.

The day and night our nurses be
That watch us in our infancy.
In their laps we play,
The world is our playground.
Our acts right and wrong at Thy court shall come to judgment;
Some be seated near Thy seat, some ever kept distant.
The toils have ended of those that have worshipped Thee,
O Nanak, their faces are lit with joyful radiance—many others they set free.

Panj nivajan vakht panj

There are five prayers
Each with a time and a name of its own.
First, truthfulness.
Second, to take only what is your due.
Third, goodwill towards all.
Fourth, pure intentions;
And praise of God, the fifth.
Let good acts be your creed: persevere with them;
Then proclaim you are a Muslim.
O Nanak, the more false the man
The more evil his power.

Kot kotee meri arja pavan peean apiao

Were I to live a million years in a cavern
Pierced neither by the sun nor the moon;
Too small to let me stretch myself,
Too small to sleep and dream;
Were my food and drink the air I breathed
(And I tried to assess Thy worth)
I would not know how great Thou art.
How then can I praise Thee?

He is the Truth, He is without form.
He is self-existent, beyond compare.
We hear of Him, then we speak of Him.
If He wills we have to know Him.
Were I to be slashed to shreds
Minced and ground to pulp
Fired in a furnace, with ashes mingled,
I would not know how great Thou art.

Were I a bird soaring through a hundred skies
Beyond the range of vision
Feeding on nothing, drinking nothing,
I would not know how great Thou art.
How then can I praise Thee?

O Nanak, had I a hundred thousand tonnes of paper
And filled the pages with the essence of learning
Pen plying with the speed of wind, dipping in an inexhaustible inkwell,
Even so
I would not know how great Thou art.
How then can I praise Thee?

Jal moh ghas mas kar mat kagad kar sar

Burn away attachment to things of the world
Crush its soot to make ink;
Use your understanding as if it were a sheet of paper,
With the pen of love
Your mind the scribe
And the guru to guide you
Write down your thoughts.

Write the Name of the Lord
Write praises of the Lord
Write that He is without end and without limit.

Brother, if you learn to write all these things
Yours will be the password at the place of reckoning.

You will be acclaimed with honour.
A joyous welcome you will receive,
On your forehead will be the mark of approval
If in the Name of the True One you truly believe.

This is the gift of grace
Idle prattle is all else.

One comes, another goes;
Some style themselves as sardars
Others are destined to beg
Yet others hold grand *darbars*.
Man will know this truth when he dies
That without the Name nothing avails
(Without the Name all else is lies).

Thy might strikes terror in my heart,
My body wastes away in fear of Thee.
Proud, titled Khans and Sultans have I seen
Reduced to dust.

O Nanak, many have I seen pack up and go
I have seen the bonds of false love cut asunder.

Tan jal bal nati bhaia, man maya moh manoor

My body is burnt to ashes and mingled with dust
My mind is rusted with attachment to worldly things;
Once again my sins pursue me
And falsehood trumpets its victory.
Without the Word we are caught in the wheel
(Of birth, death and rebirth).
Thus hath double-minded duality
Been the undoing of multitudes.
My soul, fix thy mind on the Word Divine
The Word will take thee across the waters of life.
Those who the guru's teaching do not know
Will die and be reborn, go and come, come and go.
A person is pure
If he enshrines the True Name within him.
His body is imbued with the fear of the True One
And his tongue loves the taste of truth.
He, by God's grace, is in a state of ecstasy
His body is of passions free.
The True One made the air,
From air came water
From the waters He made the three regions
In every heart He lit His lamp.
The Lord is Pure, He cannot be defiled.
He who is dyed in the colours of the Lord
Will be honoured (and remain unsullied).

The mind is the true abode of peace
Therein comes the grace of the Lord
The five elements of his body

Are tempered in the fear of the True One
The light of Truth illumines his mind.
O Nanak! His sins are forgiven
And the guru preserves his honour.

Achal chalai na chalai

He deprives of delusion
The things that delude;
He blunts the edge of the dagger
And it does not wound.
Man's mind wavers for it is full of craving;
He is safe only in the Lord's keeping.

How then light the lamp when there is no oil?
Let your body be the lamp,
From the holy books take wisdom
And use it as oil.
Let knowledge of His presence be the wick
And with the tinder of truth
Strike the spark.
Thus light you the oil-lamp
And in its light meet your Lord.

When the recording Angel claims your body
And catalogues your deeds,
Your good acts will save you from the cycle of birth and death.
If in life you have served others
Your reward shall be a place in His court.
Says Nanak: You will raise your arms in joy.

Sabhe kant maheliya saglia karah seegar

We are His wives; we adorn ourselves for Him.
We dress ourselves in bright red to gain His attention
But love is not won by bargaining; a counterfeit coin
    gilded with gold is soon found out and spells ruin.
How does a woman win the attention of the Lord?
Lord, she who is pleasing to Thy sight is in nuptial bliss;
    Thy mercy is her adornment.

The guru's word is her adornment; her body and soul are with her Lord.
With hands clasped she waits on Him; her prayer
    comes from the truthfulness of her heart.
She is immersed in His love, she lives in fear of the True One;
And when dyed with His love, her colour is fast and true.
She is counted among the followers of the Beloved.
She is recognized as one of His hand-maidens.
Her love is not sundered; the True One unites her with Himself.
Her soul is plaited with the Word
I am ever a sacrifice unto her.
She who is absorbed in the true guru becomes immortal,
    never shall she become a widow.
Her Beloved is forever handsome and renews
His youth; He does not die nor depart.
He ever enjoys His fulfilled wife; His gracious eyes
    rest on her ever-obedient person.
Truth is in the plaits of her hair, love in her dress and ornaments,
God within her is like the breath of sandal perfume,
    her chamber has the tenth gate (through which the Lord enters).

She lights the lamp of the Word, she wears God's name as her necklace.
She is beautiful amongst women of beauty; on her
    forehead she wears the jewel of love.

Her beauty and wisdom are bewitching, her love is true and infinite.
She knows no man besides her Beloved; it is only for
    the true guru that she has love and affection.

Why did you waste the dark night in sleep?
How will you pass the hours without your Lord?
Woman, your bosom shall be afire, your body burn, and your mind be aflame.
A woman not taken by her Husband wastes away her youth.
Her Husband is on her couch; but she sleeps and knows not of His presence.
I sleep while my Beloved is awake; to whom shall I turn for advice?
Sayeth Nanak, the true guru teaches how to fear and love God
And thus be united with Him.

Re man Hari seo aisee preet kar jaisee jal kamleh

My soul hearken unto me!
Love thy Lord as the lotus loves water
Buffeted by waves its affection does not falter.
Creatures that have their being in water,
Taken out of water, die.
My soul! If thou hast not such love
How wilt thou obtain release?
If the Word of the guru is within us
We shall accumulate a store of devotion.

My soul hearken unto me!
Love thy Lord as a fish loves water.
The more the water, the greater its joy,
Greater the tranquillity of its body and mind.
Without water it cannot live one watch of the day
Only God knows the anguish of its heart.

My soul hearken unto me!
Love thy Lord as the *Chatrik* loves the rain.
Although the lakes be full, the plains flooded and green
It will not drink one drop.
By God's grace, its thirst will be slaked
But destiny may doom it to die.

My soul hearken unto me!
Love thy Lord as water loves milk.
It takes on the heat, boils and evaporates before the milk can suffer.
He alone unites, He alone separates
He alone bestows true greatness.

My soul hearken unto me!
Love thy Lord as the *Chakvi* loves the sun
It sleeps not a wink for the distant sun it deems close.
The perverse of mind know not that the godly are ever in His presence.
The perverse of mind make many calculations
What the Creator does comes to pass.
Much as all desire to evaluate Him, He cannot be evaluated.
Through the teaching of the guru can He be found
And with the True One comes tranquillity.

If the true guru presents it, true love will not sunder
We are given the gift of knowledge and learn the secret of the three worlds.
If we trade in goodness, we shall not forget the Name that is pure.

Birds that fed on land and water have sported and left their feeding ground.
We are here a watch or two on borrowed time; our
    sport is also for the day and the morrow.
He whom Thou unitest with Thyself find their true abode.

Without the guru, love cannot be born
The dross of the ego cannot be rinsed away.
He who recognizes the God within
Understands the secret of the Word and is happy.

Disciples of the guru know their real selves,
No need have they for anyone's help.

Why speak of those who are already one with God?
They have the Word and are fulfilled.
The perverse of mind do not comprehend,
They are separated from God and suffer.
O Nanak! There is but one gate to the Lord's mansion
And there is no other sanctuary.

Paunai pani agni ka mel

Air, water and fire
Of these elements is our body made
Within it is the restless agitation of the mind.
It has nine doorways
The tenth is the one through which one goes to meet God.
O learned one, have you thought of this?

Everyone can discourse, speak and listen.
Only he who thinks for himself is a true scholar
And a learned divine.

The body is made of clay
The sounds that emerge are of substance airy.
Know you, O learned one,
What dies when a man does *die*?

Consciousness dies
Then dies the ego
But the soul, it dies not.

What seek you in pilgrimage to sacred rivers?
The priceless jewel is enthroned within your breast.
The learned pandit reads much, declaims much
But knows not of the treasure within.

It is not I who die.
But the demon of ignorance who is destroyed;
The soul that sustains me dies not.
Says Nanak, this is what the Lord the Creator has shown me
Now I know there is neither birth nor death.

Sun nah prabhu jeo ekaldi ban mahe

All alone am I in the wilderness
O Lord, my Husband, listen to me!
How can a wife be free of care
Unless she finds You who are free of all cares?

She cannot live without her Husband
Her nights are long and hard to endure
For sleep comes not to her,
O Lord of Love, listen to my prayer!

Only my Love cares for me, none else gives a thought to me,
Alone am I in my lamentation.
O Nanak, the fortunate woman has her tryst with her Lord

And becomes one with Him.
Without Him her life is indeed a tale of sorrow.

Akhan jivan visrai mar jaun

By prayer I live; without it I die.
The Name of the True One is hard to say
Hunger for the Name of the True One
Fulfils that hunger and sorrows fly away.

Why then forget Him, O mother of mine?
The Lord is true, His Name is Truth divine.

Praise of the True Name is a bare mustard seed (of His real greatness)
We'll speak of Him till we are weary of speech,
(We run out of words) and yet not His values reach.
If all together we exalted His nature
It would neither increase nor decrease His stature.

He does not die; He suffers no sorrow
He goes on giving, His bounty never fails,
This virtue alone hath He
None like Him there was before
None like Him shall hereafter be.

Thy bounty is as great as Thy might
Thou madest the day and also the night.
He who forgets Thee is of low birth
O Nanak! One without Name is lowest of the low-born.

Jeta sabad surat dhun teti jeta rup kaya teri

All the sounds we hear are but a part of the mighty roar of Thy torrent,
All the sights we see are but a part of Thy vast creation,
Thou art the taste (in all we taste)
Thou art the fragrance (in all that is fragrant).
O mother of mine! No other hath these qualities.
My Master is One
He is One, brother, the only One.

He is the Destroyer and the Redeemer
He gives and He takes
He regards and rejoices,
He is the granter of grace.

He is the Doer of whatever is to be done,
No one else can make that claim.
As He deals with us, so we speak of Him.
Everything doth His greatness proclaim.
In this dark age man's mind is like a brewer's vat
Filled with the sweet wine of delusion.
Sayeth humble Nanak,
This is also one of Thy many manifestations.

Simal rukh saraira ati diragh ati much

The *simal* tree is huge and straight
But if one comes to it with hope of gain
What will one get and whither turn?
Its fruit is without taste

Its flowers have no fragrance
Its leaves are of no use.
O Nanak, humility and sweetness
Are the essence of virtue and goodness.
Readily do we all pay homage to ourselves
Before others we refuse to bow.

Weigh anything in a pair of scales and see
That of greater substance does the lower go.
The wicked man bends over double
As deer-slayer shooting his dart.
What use is bending or bowing of head
When you bow not your heart?

Daya kapah santokh soot jat gandhi sat vat

When making the sacred thread, the *Janeau*,
See that following rules you pursue.
Out of the cotton of compassion
Spin the thread of tranquillity
Let continence be the knot
And virtue the twist thereon.
O pandit, if such a sacred thread there be
Around our neck, we shall wear it willingly.

A thread so made will not break
It will not get dirty, be burnt or lost.
O Nanak, thou shall see
Those who wear this shall blessed be.

For four cowrie shells this thread is bought
A square is marked for the ceremony.
The Brahmin whispers a *mantra* in the ear
And thus becomes the guru and teacher.
But when the wearer dies, cast away is his thread
And threadless he goes on his voyage ahead.

Je kar sootak manneeai sab tai sootak hoe

Once we say: This is pure, this unclean,
See that in all things there is life unseen.
There are worms in wood and cowdung cakes,
There is life in the corn ground into bread.
There is life in the water which turns plants green.
How then be clean when impurity is over the kitchen spread?

O Nanak, not thus are things impure purified
Wash them with divine knowledge instead.
Impurity of the mind is greed,
Of tongue, untruth
Impurity of the eye is coveting
Another's wealth, his wife, her comeliness;
Impurity of the ears is listening to calumny.
O Nanak, thus does the fettered soul
Wing its way to the city of doom.

Apey bhandey sajeean apey pooran dey

God gives shape to human vessels
And God fills them with what He wills

Into some He pours milk
Others He makes simmer on the hearths,
Some are destined to sleep on soft couches
Others spend their nights keeping a vigil,
He saves those whom He wills.

Amli amal na ambdai machi neer na hoe

To the opium addict there is nothing like opium.
To the fish water is everything.
Those imbued with the Name of their Lord
Find every prospect pleasing.

May every moment of my life be a sacrifice to Thy Name, O my Master!

My Master is like a tree that beareth fruit
The Name of the fruit is nectar
Those who drink its juice are truly fulfilled
May my life be sacrificed to them!

Thou livest amongst all creatures
Yet I see Thee not;
How can the thirsty their thirst slake,
If a wall separates them from the like?

Nanak is Thy tradesman;
Thou art my Master and my goods.
My mind would rid itself of delusion
If to Thee I addressed my prayers
And to Thee my petition.

Mori run jhun laya, bhainey savan aya

Sweet sound of water gurgling down the water-spout
(The peacock's shrill, exultant cry)
Sister, it's *savan*, the month of rain!
Beloved Thine eyes bind me in a spell
(They pierce through me like daggers)
They fill my heart with greed and longing;
For one glimpse of Thee I'll give my life
For Thy Name may I be a sacrifice.
When Thou art mine, my heart fills with pride,
What can I be proud of if Thou art not with me?
Woman, smash thy bangles on thy bedstead.

Break thy arms, break the arms of thy couch;
Thy adornments hold no charms
Thy Lord is in another's arms.

The Lord liked not thy bangle-seller
Thy bracelets and glass bangles He doth spurn
Arms that do not the Lord's neck embrace
With anguish shall forever burn.
All my friends have gone to their lovers
I feel wretched, whose door shall I seek?
Friends, of proven virtue and fair am I
Lord, does nothing about me find favour in Thine eye?

I plaited my tresses,
With vermilion daubed the parting of my hair
And went to Him
But with me He would not lie.
My heart is grief-stricken, I could die.
I wept, and the world wept with me.

Even birds of the forest cried,
Only my soul torn out of my body shed not a tear,
Nay, my soul which separated me from my Beloved shed not a tear.
In a dream He came to me
(I woke) and He was gone.
I wept a flood of tears.
Beloved I cannot come to Thee,
No messenger will take my message;
Blessed sleep come thou back to me,
That in my dreams my Lover I again may see!
Nanak, what wilt thou give the messenger
Who brings thee a message from thy Master?
I'll sever my head to make a seat for him;
Headless though I be, I'll continue to serve him.
Why then do I not die? Why not give away my life?
My Husband is estranged from me and has taken another wife!

ARTI: Gagan mai thal ravi chand dipak banai

The firmament is Thy salver
The sun and moon Thy lamps;
The galaxy of stars as pearls strewn.
A mountain of sandal is Thy joss-stick
Breezes that blow Thy fan;
All the woods and vegetation
All flowers that bloom
Take their colours from Thy light.

Thus we wave the salver of lamps
How beautiful is this ritual!

Thou art the destroyer of the cycle of birth, death and rebirth.
In Thy temple echo beats the drum unstruck by hands.

A thousand eyes hast Thou, yet no eye hast Thou.
A thousand shapes hast Thou, yet no shape hast Thou.
A thousand feet hast Thou, yet no foot hast Thou.
A thousand nostrils hast Thou, yet no nose hast Thou.
These are miracles that have bewitched my heart.

Thine is the light in every lamp.
Thine the radiance in all that is radiant.
The guru's teaching illumines our minds.
What pleases Him is the true worship of lamps.

As the honey bee seeks honey in flowers
My soul which is ever athirst,
Seeks Thy lotus feet
To slake its thirst for nectar.

Lord, show Thy mercy
Give Nanak the water he seeks.
He like the sarang cries for rain
Let him forever abide in Thy Name.

Ih tan maya pahia pyarey leetda lab rangae

Dear friend, I am like one drowned in a dyer's vat
Brimful with delusions of maya
I have become like a cloth dyed with greed.

Dear friend, the colour of my cloak
Pleases not the Lord my Groom.
How then shall I who am His bride,
Be invited to His nuptial couch?

Let my life be a sacrifice unto Thee, O Merciful One!
Let my life be a sacrifice!
Let my life be a sacrifice to those who worship Thy Name.
Yea, let my life be sacrificed to them a hundred times.

Dear friend, if the body be like a dyer's vat
We must fill it with the madder of the Lord's Name;
The Divine Dyer will dye it in hues none hath ever seen.

Dear friend, she whose garment is thus dyed
Hath the Lord her Groom by her side.
Nanak prays for the dust of her feet.

The Lord weaves the cloth and dyes it.
He Himself appraises the colours.
Sayeth Nanak, if the woman thus adorned please Him
He will be gracious and take her unto Himself.

Sau ulame dinai key rati milan sahans

The day's hundred regrets
By night multiply tenfold;
As a swan instead of feeding on pearls
(Which are its real sustenance)
Pecks at carrion

So man forgets to sing hosannas to his God
(Which are the real sustenance for his soul
And turns instead to the fleshpots of the world).
Cursed be the life thus wasted
In stuffing food and increasing the paunch.
The Name of the True One changes not; that much we know
All else, sayeth Nanak, turns from friend to foe.

THE TWELVE MONTHS

(The practice of composing lyrics according to the twelve months of the year, to highlight human emotions and make spiritual or moral messages accessible to people, was common among Indian poets. Guru Nanak's Bara Maha, *composed in Tukhari raga, is the most highly rated in the Punjabi language. It is believed to be among the last of the Guru's compositions.)*

Chet (March–April)

Chet basant bhala bhavar suhavre

It is the month of Chet,
It is spring. All is seemly—
The humming bumble-bee
And the woodland in flower—
But there is a sorrow in my soul.

The Lord, my Master is away.
If the Husband comes not home, how can a wife
Find peace of mind?

Sorrows of separation waste away the body.
The *Koel* calls in the mango grove,
Its notes are full of joy.
Why then the sorrow in my soul?
The bumble-bee hovers about the blossoming bough,
O mother of mine, it is like death to me,
For there is a sorrow in my soul.

Nanak says: When the Lord her Master comes home to her,
       Blessed is then the month of Chet.

Vaisakh (April–May)

Vaisakh bhala sakha ves kare

In beauteous Vaisakh the bough adorns itself anew,
The wife awaits the coming of her Lord,
Her eyes fixed on the door.
'My Love, You alone can help me across
The turbulent waters of life. Come home.
Without You I am worthless as a broken shell.
When You look upon me with favour, Love,
And our eyes mingle;
Then shall I become priceless beyond compare.'

Nanak says: 'Where seek you the Lord?
Whom are you awaiting?
You have not far to go to find Him.
He is within you, you are His mansion.
If your body and soul yearn for the Lord,
The Lord shall love you and Vaisakh be beautiful.'

Jeth (May–June)

Mah Jeth bhala pritam kiun bisrai

Why forget the Beloved in the month of Jeth
When the land shimmers in the summer's heat?
Grant me the Virtues, O Lord,
As win favour in Your eyes.
You are free from all attachment
And live in Truth.
And I am lowly, humble, helpless.
How shall I approach You?
How find the haven of peace?

Says Nanak: She who knows the Lord
Becomes like the Lord.
She knows Him
By treading the path of virtue.

Asad (June–July)

Asad bhala suraj gagan tape

In Asad the Sun scorches.
The sky is hot
The earth burns like an oven,
Waters give up their vapours.
It burns and scorches relentlessly in the month of Asad.
The Sun's chariot passes the noon's sky
The wife watches the shadow creep across the courtyard.

And the cicada calls from the glades.
The beloved seeks the cool of the evening.
If the comfort she seeks be in falsehood,
There will be sorrow in store for her.
If it be in truth,
Hers will be a life of joy.

Says Nanak: Life and life's end are at the will of the Lord
            To Him have I surrendered my soul.

Savan (July–August)

Savan sars mana ghan varsai

The season of rain has come.
My heart is full of joy,
My body and soul yearn for the Master.
But He is away in foreign lands
If He return not, I shall die pining for Him.

The lightning strikes terror in my heart.
I am alone in my courtyard
In solitude and sorrow.
O Mother of mine, I stand on the brink of death,
Without the Lord I have no hunger or sleep
I cannot suffer the clothes on my body.

Nanak says: She alone is blest
            Who becomes One with the Lord.

Bhadon (August–September)

Bhadon bharm bhuli bhar joban pachtani

Lost in the maze of falsehood
I waste my full-bloom youth.
River and land are one expanse of water
For it is the glad season of the rains.
It rains.
The nights are dark.
There is no peace for me.
Frogs croak in contentment.
Peacocks cry with joy.
The *papeeha* calls peeooh, peeooh.
The fangs of serpents that crawl,
The bite of mosquitoes that fly,
Are full of venom.

The seas have burst their bounds in the ecstasy of fulfilment.
I alone am bereft of joy,
Whither shall I go?
How shall I find Him?

Nanak says: Ask of the Guru the way
            He knows the path which leads to the Lord.

Asan (September–October)

Asun au pira sadhan jhur mui

O Master, come to me,
I waste and will die.
If the Master wills,

I shall meet Him.
If He wills not,
I am lost utterly.
I took the path of falsehood,
And the Master forsook me,
Age has greyed my locks
I have lived many winters
The fires of hell still lie ahead,
And I am afraid.

The bough remains ever green
For the sap that moves within
Night and day, renews life.
If the Name of the Lord courses in your veins,
Life and hope will for ever be green.
Meditate calmly on the Name.
That which ripens slowly ripens best.

Nanak says: Come now, my Love,
           Even the Guru pleads for me.

Katak (October–November)

Katak kirat paiya jo prabh bhae

What pleases the Lord
Is all I merit.
The lamp of wisdom burns steadily
If the oil that feeds it
Be reality.
If the oil that feeds the lamp be Love
The beloved will meet the Lord and find fulfilment.

Full of faults, she is caught
In the cycle of birth and death
And finds no favour with the Lord.
Good deeds alone will end her sorrow.

Those who are granted the worship of Your Name
Hope to meet You in Your mansion.

Nanak says: O Lord till You grant us Your vision
        And break the bonds of superstition,
        One watch of day will drag like half a year.

Maghar (November–December)

Maghar mah bhala harigun ank smavai

The month of Maghar is bliss
To her who is lost in the Lord
For she is the virtuous one
And loves the Lord Eternal.

He Who is eternal, omniscient, wise is also the Master of destiny.
The world is in turmoil without faith.
She who has knowledge and contemplates on Him
Loses herself in Him.
By His grace she loves the Lord.

Proclaim the name of Rama in song and dance and verse,
And sorrow will flee away.

Nanak says: Only she is loved
        Who prays to her Lord
        With her heart.

Pokh (December–January)

Pokh tukhar pare van trin ras sokhai

As the winter snow
Freezes the sap in tree and bush,
The absence of the Lord
Blights the body and the soul.
O Lord why do You not come?

He who gives life to the world
Him do I praise through the Guru's word.
His light is in all life born
Of the egg or womb or sweat or seed.
O Merciful Master, O Bounteous You
Grant me Your vision
That I may find salvation.

Nanak says: She who is in love with the Lord
        Is infused with grace.

Magh (January–February)

Magh punit bhai tirath antar jania

The Lord has entered my being.
I make pilgrimage within myself and am purified.
I met Him.
He found me good
And let me lose myself in Him.
'Beloved! If you find me fair
My pilgrimage is made,
I am cleansed.

57

More than the sacred waters of Ganga, Yamuna
    and Tribeni mingled at the Sangam;
More than the seven seas,
More than charity, almsgiving and prayer
Is the knowledge of Eternity that is the Lord.'

Nanak says: He who has worshipped the Great Giver of life
                Has earned more merit than those who
                    bathe at the sixty and eight places of pilgrimage.

Phalgun (February–March)

Phalgun man rehsi prem subhae

She whose heart is full of love
Is ever in full bloom.
Joy is hers for she has no love of self.
Only those who love You
Conquer love of self.
Come, Lord, and abide in me.

Many a garment did I wear,
The Master willed not and
His palace was barred to me.
When He wanted me, I went
With garlands and strings of jewels and raiment of finery.

Nanak says: A bride welcomed in the Master's mansion
                Has found her true Love.

GURU
ANGAD DEV
{1504–1552}

There are sixty-two hymns by Guru Angad in the Adi Granth.

Jo sir saeen na nivai so sir deejai daar

Cut off the head, O Nanak,
That bows not to the Lord;
Burn the wretched flesh
That feels not the pain of separation.

Akhin bajhon vekhna bin kana sunana

To see without eyes,
Without ears, hear,
To walk without feet,
Without hands, work,
To speak without a tongue—
Thus living, yet detached from life.

O Nanak, if you follow the word of your Master
You shall surely meet Him.

Ihu jagu sachche ki hai kothari

All the world is His dwelling place; the True One among us resides.
Whom He wills He makes one with Himself, whom He wills He destroys;
By His will is one rid of illusion, by His will another ensnared.
And which one of us can know who shall receive His grace?
Says Nanak, he alone finds the Supreme Guru, whose mind He illumines.

GURU
AMAR DAS

{1479–1574}

There are 907 hymns by Guru Amar Das in the Adi Granth.

Manmukh lok samjhayiai kadon samjhaya jae

If you preach to the wicked
Can you turn them from their wicked ways?
They will not mingle with the good however much you try
But will tread their own wayward paths
For such is their desert.

There are two ways:
Love of the Lord and love of gold.
By His ordinance alone one finds the right path.
The good conquer their sinfulness
And the touchstone of the Guru's word
Declares them pure.

It is with the mind we must battle,
With the mind we must come to terms
And with the mind make peace.
The mind gets what it wills
By the power of Truth and love of the word.

Drink deep of the nectar that is the Name
And let your deeds be righteous.
If your battles are not with your own mind
But with others
You will have wasted your life.

The wicked surrender to their wilful minds
Their ways are false, their reward evil.
The good win their battles over their minds
For they have their thoughts fixed on God.

Nanak says: The good through Truth attain salvation
           The wicked escape not the cycle of birth and death.

Maya kis no akhiai, kya maya karm kamae?

What is maya? What acts spring from it?
The snare of joy and sorrow in which our lives are caught,
The thought of self that moves us to action.
Without the word there is no wisdom,
Nothing to tear apart maya's veil of illusion,
Nothing to exorcise the ego.
Without love you cannot be a devotee,
Without the word, you will find no rest.
It is the word alone that conquers self
And destroys illusion.
The pious receive the gift of the Name
By gentle ways and good conduct.

Without the Guru one cannot tell
The good from the bad.

Without goodness, prayer has no meaning.
If God is in the heart
He can be met face to face.
He comes as gently as comes sleep.

O Nanak, raise your voice in praise of the Guru
By His grace you shall attain salvation.

Kajal phul tambol ras

She put black in her eyes, flowers in her hair,
With betel leaves sweetened her breath and her lips stained;
But the Lord came not to her bed
All her adornments were in vain.

Woman and man who just live together, speak not of them as truly wed,
When in two bodies a single light burns, then are man and woman truly wed.

Without the fear of the Lord
One cannot be a true devotee
For one has no love of the Name.
Love is born on meeting the true Guru.
Fear and love together give the proper hue
They kill the hunger of the ego
And with His Name, body and soul imbue.
Body and Soul thus cleansed, made of beauty rare
Give to the Lord, the Destroyer of Evil.
Both fear and love to him the Lord does give
Who in this world do truthfully live.

Anandu bhaiya meri mayi

Mother, my heart is full of joy
For I have found my true guru;
I found the true guru following the gentle path of *sahaj*
My heart resounds with cries of felicitation
Jewel-like ragas and their families of fairy-like houris
Have come to sing hymns of praise;
They within whom Hari resides, divine hymns sing
Says Nanak, I have attained bliss because the true guru I did find.

Ae man meriya tun sadaa rahe Hari naale

My heart, ever abide with the Lord Hari
Abide with the Lord and forget all your misery;
Gathering you within Himself
He will sort out all your affairs.
In every way He is your master
Why then let Him out of your mind?
Says Nanak, my mind, forever with the Hari abide.

Sache sahiba kiya nahi ghar tere

Master true, what is it that is not in Your house?
There is everything there
Only those You choose to give find it.
Lord grant me the gift of ever singing Your praise
So Your name gets imprinted on my mind.

The hearts of those wherein dwells the name
Always resound with hymns of praise
Asks Nanak, true Lord what is there not found in Your house?

Sacha nam mera adharo

Name of the true Lord is my support
With the true name's help, I lost all my hungers
It gave me peace of mind, contentment and fulfilled all my desires
Forever may my life be sacrificed to the guru who is so great
Says Nanak, ye men of God, cherish his words
For the name of the true one is my mainstay.

Vaje panch sabad titu dhari sabhage

All five kinds of musical instruments
Play in the hearts of the blessed;
In their blessed homes plays celestial music
Where God has infused his magic and might.
And the five evils (lust, anger, greed, self-love and
    arrogance) are suppressed
And the fear of death is no more
Only those who were predestined
Attach themselves and the true name find.
Says Nanak, there is always happiness
Where uninterrupted divine music plays.

Kalao masaajni ki-aa sadaeai hirdai hi likh leho

Why need you pen and ink? Write upon your heart.
Dye yourself in the colour of the Lord, and you are his forever.
Pen and ink will not endure, nor even what was written.
O Nanak, love of the Lord shall not perish; it is a gift from the True One.

GURU
RAM DAS
{1534–1581}

There are 679 hymns by Guru Ram Das in the Adi Granth.

Gur satgur ka jo sikh akhae

He who would call himself the disciple of the Guru, the True Guru,
Should rise early and meditate on Hari who is God.
He should bathe in the 'nectar-pool'
And labour during the day.
He should hear the words of the Guru his teacher
And repeat the names of Hari
For then will his sins be forgiven and his suffering cease.
As the day advances, let him sing the hymns of the Guru
And keep the Lord in his mind in all he does.
He that repeats the name of Hari with every breath
And with every morsel that he eats
He is the real Sikh, him the Guru loves.
He to whom the Lord is gracious
Listens to the Guru's teaching and becomes his disciple.
Nanak, your servant begs for the dust of the feet of Sikhs
Who worship and lead others to the path of worship.

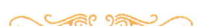

Mero sundar kaho milai kit gali?

What shall I do to meet my Love?
O you who worship Him show the way
Let me follow in your footsteps.
The path that leads to Him is of obedience to Love's commandments,
Of treasuring them in the heart.
They matter not: your untidy scattered locks,
Your short stature, your bent and ugly body.
If you find favour in His eyes
You shall be beautiful and sit beside Him.

Our Lord is the One Lord
And we his consorts.
She who His beloved is
Is the best of wives.

O Nanak, why need you bother yourself
If the Lord wills, He will show the way.

Har ke jan satgur satpurkha

We seekers of the Lord beseech you our true guru,
To you who is truth personified we pray;
We are but worms and vermin seeking your protection,
Be merciful, illumine our hearts with your name.

My friend and mentor, suffuse my heart with the name of Rama;
Let teachings of the guru my life sustain
Let singing praises of the Lord show me the way
And be my evensong.

Men of the Lord are fortune's favourites
They are ever firm in their faith
And ever thirst for the Lord.
Finding the elixir of the Lord's name
Their thirsts are slaked.
In the company of holy men
His virtues they praise.

Most unfortunate are those,
And caught in shackles of life and death,
Who have not tasted the nectar of His name.
Those who sought not the Lord's protection
Nor the holy congregation,
Are damned in this life and for lives to come.

Those devotees blessed with the guru's companionship,
Bear marks of blessed fate on their foreheads.
Twice blessed is that congregation
Where the nectar of the Lord's name is found.
There, says Nanak,
The Lord's name is illumined and enlightenment found.

So purakh niranjan, hari purakh niranjan

Our Lord is without blemish, our Lord is untainted by illusion
He is beyond comprehension, endless and beyond reach;
All worship You, the real author of all creation;
All creatures are created by You, You are their provider and giver;
O men of God, ponder over Him! He is the remover of all sorrows;
He himself the Lord, and the servant,
Says Nanak, of what worth is a mere human?

You dwell in every body, flowing uninterrupted,
You are the only one in every one;
Some you endow with riches, others you reduce to beggary,
It is all a part of your inscrutable design;
You are the giver,
You yourself the decider of how it is spent
I know not any other like you;
You are the infinite God, your expanse unknown,
How can I put your qualities in words?
Whoever serves you, on him will Nanak sacrifice his life.

Those who meditate on you, those who worship you,
Will live in peace for all their lives;
Those who meditate on you, will gain salvation
And be freed from the noose of Yama;
Those who worship the Lord who is without fear
They will themselves be freed of fear;
Those who serve the Lord
Will merge in the person of the Lord;
Twice blessed are they who contemplate God
Nanak will give his life for them.
The treasury of your worship is beyond count
Your worshippers worship you in infinite ways;
Worship you who are infinite and without end;
Many are the ways to worship you
Many forms of penance and endless the forms of prayer;
Many a sacred text is read,
Many a way to serve you, including the six Karmas;
Says your slave Nanak, those worshippers are best
Who please the Lord and by Him are blest.

You are the primal Lord, creator beyond reach
There is none equal to you;

From age to age you are the only one
Forever the only one who gives stability;
What pleases you comes to pass
What you do comes to be;
You created all that exists
You will take it all back as you will;
Your slave Nanak sings your praises
Who knows all that is worth knowing.

Toon karta sachiar mainda saeen

You are the true Creator, you are my Master
What pleases you will come to pass,
What you give, I receive.

All that exists belongs to you
You are worshipped for your creation;
To those you are pleased with,
You grant the jewel of your name.
Men of God find it, followers of Mammon lose it;
You abandon the worldly, clasp the godly to your bosom.

You are the mighty river, all within you is contained
Without you nothing exists;
All living creatures are your play things
Some get separated from you
Others by your grace merge in you.

Those you give the gift of wisdom do you appraise
And forever sing songs in your praise.

He who serves you, finds peace of mind
And in the Lord, he gently a place finds.

You are the Creator, you the executor
There is none besides you,
You create and keep everything in your sight.
Says your slave Nanak, for the godly you came to light.

GURU
ARJAN DEV
{1563–1606}

Guru Arjan's 2,218 hymns are the largest single
contribution to the Adi Granth.

Prit lagi tis sach sion marai na avai jae

I love Him who is the Truth.
He dies not; nor is reborn to die again.
I flee from Him but He does not forsake me,
He is in all our hearts.

He knows the sorrows of the poor,
He destroys their pain and suffering,
He upholds those who serve Him.

This wondrous form is the Formless One
The Guru took me to meet Him, O Mother.

Listen, my brothers, befriend Him
Shun the love that is maya's snare
For none that love maya are happy.

He knows all
He is the Great Giver

He is serene
He is charitable
He is the true friend and helper
He is very great
He towers above all
And is limitless.

He has no childhood, no old age
His Court and His Commandments are Eternal.
What we beg, He grants.
He is the hope of those without hope.

One vision of Him destroys all sin
And our soul and body find tranquillity.
With single-mindedness meditate on the One
And the mind's illusions will be dispelled.

He is the treasury of goodness
Ever youthful He is
And full of charity.
Worship Him all the time
Forget Him not night or day.

Those who are His chosen
Are befriended by Him.
I dedicate my body, soul, and my possessions,
And sacrifice my life to Him.

He sees and hears all
He dwells in the recesses of our hearts.
Even the ones who show Him no gratitude
Are helped by Him.
Nanak's God is ever forgiving.

Ja ko muskal at banai dhoi koi na dei

When troubles come and you have no one to turn to
When enemies are at your heels and your kinsmen desert you
When hope is fled, all hope shattered
Let your thoughts turn to Him who is your Maker
And no ill wind will harm you.

The Master is the strength of the feeble.
He does not come and go, He is forever where He is.
The Guru's words shall reveal the truth to you.

When you are weak and frail,
Without clothes, without food,
When no one drops a coin in your apron
Nor gives you comfort.
When no one helps you and you succeed not in your actions
Let your thoughts turn to Him who is your Maker
And your affairs will forever go well.

When cares crowd upon you
When your body is foul with disease
When you are obsessed with thoughts of your wife and your kinsmen
Are sometimes happy and sometimes sad,
When restless and agitated you wander in all directions
Without a moment's rest, without a moment's sleep
Let your thoughts turn to Him who is your Maker,
And your body and mind will forever be whole.

When lust, anger, and attachment have you captive
And full of greed you are ever wanting, covetous,
When you have committed the four sins
(Drunk wine, thieved, fornicated and killed)

And in the company of devils have become a devil,
When neither books of wisdom nor songs nor hymns of praise
Fall upon your ears
Let your thoughts turn to Him who is your Maker
And in the twinkling of an eye will you be saved.

Books of wisdom you might know by heart, and recite
Prayers and practise the penances of the Yogis, all pilgrimages undertake
And twice perform the six good acts
(Learn and impart learning to others,
Sacrifice and make others give in sacrifice
Give alms and accept charity),
Bathe in holy water and do worship.
If you love not the Lord with all your being,
It is all in vain and for you there is nothing but hell.

Empires, kingdoms, and baronies may be yours
And the wherewithal of power and pleasure.
You may own orchards, beautiful and bountiful,
And have power over others without any limit
And indulge in sports and pastimes to keep yourself amused.
If your thoughts turn not to Him who is your Maker
Yours will be the rebirth as a serpent.

You may have much wealth,
Live well and have gentle ways
Love deep your mother and father, sons, brothers and friends,
Own armies of footmen and archers, and many to bow to you in salutation,
Many to shout 'Long may you live.'
If your thoughts turn not to Him who is your Maker
You shall surely be dragged down to hell.

Your body may be free of fever and without sores,
Your mind free of cares and affliction.
Without ever the thought of death
Night and day you may enjoy yourself
And take everything as your own
Without any reserve or hesitation.
If your thoughts turn not to Him who is your Maker
For you will be in the servitude of hell's demons.

Those to whom the Creator is merciful
Is given the company of holy men,
The more they are with such companions
The more they love Him.
He is the Lord of good and evil
There is none other than Him.
O Nanak, only by His Grace will you find Him,
The True Guru, whose Name is Truth.

Tun per sakh teri phuli

You are the tree,
And the world its branches.
You were unknown
And You made Yourself manifest.
You are the ocean,
You the bubbles, You the foam;
There is nothing that is without You.
You are the string,
You the beads strung on it;
You the knot and the central bead of the rosary.
The beginning and the end and the middle

Are You; none else is there beside You.
You are *nirgun*, transcending all attributes,
You are *sargun*, teeming with attributes,
You are the Giver of all joy,
You are without desire
Yet the passionate colouring in all desire
You symbolize.
You alone know Your ways
You alone comprehend Yourself.

You are the Lord
You His servitor
You the secret, You its revelation.
Nanak, your servant, shall ever sing of You
If You grant him a little grace.

Tun mera pita, tun hain mera mata

You are my Father
You my Mother
You are my Kinsman
And my Brother.
Everywhere You are my Protector
What reason have I to harbour fear?

By Your grace I recognise You.
You are my Support
You are my Pride
I know of no other beside You.
The world is but an arena for Your sport.

You are the Creator of life and matter
The Dispenser of all destiny.
All that comes to pass is by Your decree;
We have no hand in the performance.

Those that have pondered on Your nature
Have found great bliss.
By singing Your praise
My heart has found peace and comfort.
O Nanak, the Almighty Guru Himself rejoices,
Since you have won the great battle.

Kin bidh kusal hot mere bhai

Tell me brother, how does one find peace?
How to find the God, Rama, who is our help?
Maya has spread its net everywhere to catch us.
There is no happiness in the home of the humble
Nor in the lofty mansions of the rich.
In false pursuits we waste our lives
We joy in the possession of horses and elephants
In armies and ministers and retinues of servants,
Thus do we put the halter round our necks
And fasten the noose of the 'I am'.
We wander in all directions seeking power
We sport in the company of damsels
And being beggars
Dream ourselves to be kings.
One truth has the True Guru told me
What the Lord does His followers should accept as the best.

Nanak, the servant, says: By killing thoughts of self and merging in Him
Is found peace, O brother of mine.
Only thus we find God who is Rama.

Anik jatan nahi hot chhut-kaara

It is not through trickery that one gets release
However many the tricks one tries.
Much learning only increases the load of sorrows.
It is only service and the love of God
That takes one with honour to His Court.
O Soul of mine! If you make the name of the Lord your shelter
No ill-wind shall harm you.

As the sight of a boat on stormy seas
As the light of a lamp in the dark
As the warmth of fire in winter's cold
Does prayer bring solace to the soul.

The thirst of your soul will be quenched
Your hopes fulfilled
Your mind will cease to wander
For nectar is the name of the Lord
And the friendship of godly men.
The healing balm of prayer is given only to him
To whom the Lord is gracious and grants the boon.
Those whose hearts echo the name of the Lord Hari
Their sorrow and pain, O Nanak, are banished.

Bhuj bal bir brahma sukh sagar

O Lord of Mighty Arms,
Creator of all things,
O Ocean of peace!
Take me by my hand and raise me
Who am fallen in a pit.

My ears hear not
My eyes have lost their light
I am crippled, afflicted
Like a leper I come stumbling to Your door
And cry for help.
You are the Lord of the fallen,
Above You there is no Lord
O Compassionate One,
You are my Companion, Friend, Father and Mother.
Let Nanak bear the imprint of Your feet in his heart.
Let Your saints ferry me across the fearful ocean of life.

Prithmai tyagi haumai rit

I discarded the love of self
And the ways of the world,
I gave up distinction between friend and foe
And was blessed with knowledge to recognize the godly.
In the cave of *sahaj* I sat in meditation
Saw the light, heard divine music
And pondered over the word in utter bliss.
I was the blessed bride taken by the Lord.

Nanak, your servant who has thought much about this, says:
He who listens and then acts
Lands safely on the other shore.
For him there is no more birth and death, no more coming and going.
With the Hari he is one forever.

Gun avgun mero kachu na bichario

My merits and demerits You did not reckon
Nor looked upon my face, complexion or adornment.
I knew no winsome ways nor manner of deportment
But You took me by the hand and drew me to Your bed.
Listen my friends—My Groom has become my Master
He puts his hand upon my forehead and calls me His own.
What know the foolish men of the world?
Now has my union been consummated
My Groom knows my sorrows and has dispelled them.
The moonlight shines in my courtyard
Night and day I live in ecstasy with my Love.
My raiments are redder than the rose
I glitter with jewels and garlands of flowers.
My Love looks at me and I have the wealth of the world.
I have no fear of the wicked demons.
I am eternally happy and full of joy—
I have found Truth in my home.

Says Nanak: She who has adorned herself for the Lord
          Hers is the true consummation.

Jaise kirsan bovai kirsani

As a farmer sows his field
And mows it at his will
Be it green or ripe,
So does the Lord take at His will
All that is born
And dies.
Only the worshipper of Govind is immortal.
The day is followed by the night
The night passes and comes the dawn,
But the wretched sleep in maya's delusion,
Only the rare ones are roused
By the Grace of the Guru.
O Nanak, forever sing praise of the Lord
It cleanses the heart and illumines the face.

Jan tun sahib tan bhau keha

What fear have I when You are my Master,
Who else shall I worship?
If I have You, I have everything,
I look to no other.
Lord, much venom have I seen in the world,
You are my Shepherd, my Protector,
Your Name is my comfort
You know the anguish in my heart
To whom shall I tell my sorrow?
Without Your Name the world is in turmoil,

Only those who take Your Name find peace.
What shall I say? Who will listen to me?
The Lord alone can speak.

You are the Maker.
Forever and ever You are my hope,
In making me great, You magnify Your greatness,
Now and always it is You I will worship.

Nanak's Lord is the constant Giver of Joy.
His Name is my only strength.

Subh chintan gobind raman, nirmal sadhu sang

O Lord, grant me these: purity of thought,
Will to worship, company of godly men,
And the power never to forget You for even a moment.

The night is damp with drops of dew
Stars twinkle in the sky,
Those beloved of the Lord are risen
For those the Lord loves are ever awake.
Night and day His Name is on their lips
In their hearts rest His lotus feet
Their thoughts never stray from Him.

Abandon pride and lust, they silt the mind
And smother it in the smoke of sorrow.
Nanak says, those that love the Lord are ever awake.

Meri sejarye adambar baniya

Upon my bed I awaited His coming,
My heart leaped with joy when I heard His footsteps.
He came to me, He Who is my Lord and Master.
My desires were fulfilled, I was with joy replete.
He took me in His arms, limb to limb we lay
And my anguish was gone.
My life, my soul, my body were all refreshed.
My wishes were granted; I worshipped Him.
Blessed was the hour I met Him.
Says Nanak: I have met the Lord of Lakshmi
And joy all is mine.

My companions ask me, by what signs did I know He was my Master?
Filled with ecstasy, I could not utter a word in reply.
His goodness is profound and hidden.
Even books of wisdom know not His dimensions.
With love worship Him and meditate on His Name
And ever let your voice be raised in His praise.
Our Lord is with virtues replete, His knowledge is supreme and complete.

Says Nanak, she who is filled with His love
Goes gently to His bed to rest.

Nadi tarandri mainda khoj na khumbe

Deep the waters of the stream,
I cannot swim, my feet no foothold find.
I shall ferry across for I am full of love

On the Lord's feet is fixed my mind.
O Nanak, my love is the Boatman.

Only them will I call my friends
At whose sight evil thoughts disappear;
I have sought them over all the world,
O Nanak, such men are very rare.

Let the Master be in your thoughts,
His worshippers have seen Him.
Keep the company of godly men
Then shall your sorrows end, your heart be clean.

The saintly break the fetters
At their sight devils scatter and hide,
They make us fall in love with Him
By Whose Will we all abide.

High is His seat, the highest of all;
It is beyond reach, there is nothing beyond it.
Day and night your hands in prayer join
With every breath bring the Lord to mind.
If He be gracious, He shall grant us the company of the godly.

Bar vidanre humas dhumas

Dense and terrifying is the forest,
Petrifying the stillness before the storm,
Screams of terror assail the wayfarers' ears.
You are our Leader; I hold tight the rope and follow
And thus, O Nanak, traverse the wild woodland.

Those in whose company our voices rise in prayer
Are verily our true companions.
O Nanak, shun the friendship of those
Who think of nothing but themselves.

That time is auspicious when we enter the presence of the True Guru
When we befriend the godly and sorrows do not assail us
When we find blessed rest and escape the cycle of birth and death;
For then we see the One Creator wherever we turn our gaze
We know the supreme wisdom of turning our thoughts on God
We know that the best speech is the words of prayer
We know His commandments and find joy in submission.
Such the Lord treasures, for such are of the true mint.

Bajigar jaise baji pae

As a performing juggler
Acts many parts, wears many disguises
And takes off his mask when the show is done
So is our Creator one, the only One.

What forms he brings into being
And then does banish?
From whence do they come
Where do they vanish?
Countless waves rise from the waters
Many an ornament is made from gold,
Whenever a seed is sown,
It ripens into many fruits, though the seed is one.

The same Light of Heaven is reflected in water
In a hundred pitchers contained,
The pitchers may burst
But the light remains.

Maya deludes, it creates greed and desire,
When freed of delusion we see
The Creator is One.
He is immortal, He does not die.
He did not come, He will not go.
I have met the Guru
He cleansed my mind of the ego.
Says Nanak: So was I saved
Thus did I achieve supreme salvation.

Umkio hio milan prabh tain

My heart leapt up to behold the Lord
I heard of His coming, in my heart made His cot,
I went out to meet my Beloved
I wandered everywhere but saw Him not.

O poor heart, how wilt thou get peace of mind?
I will give my life if the Lord I find.

One couch is spread for the Lord and wife.
She slumbers, Her Lord awaits ever awake
But like one drunk she sleeps.
If the Lord embrace her, she too will wake.

I am without hope, many days have passed
In many lands and continents did I seek Him.
I cannot live if I clasp not His blessed feet
If He be kind, my fortune will turn and we shall meet.

He was good and gave me the company of the true
And my restless wanderings did then cease.
In my house I found my Lord
All my adornments do Him please.
Says Nanak: The Guru has lifted illusion's veil.
   Whichever way I turn, O brother, I see my Lord
The doors of ignorance are thrown asunder
The restless mind has ceased to wander.

Ghar meh thakar nadar na avai

The Master is in the home, but we do not see Him
His image in stone round our necks we wear
Deluded by maya everywhere we wander
Churn water in hope of butter, kill ourselves with
The stone that we the Master call
That stone itself will be our fall.

Sinners we are, to our Master's salt untrue
We cannot cross in a boat that of stone is made.
Nanak met the Guru and then knew his Master
He pervades the earth, the sky and water.

Ek rup saglo pasara

He is One but does in all things pervade
He is the merchandise, His is the trade.
This truth only the rare ones learn
He is present whichever way we turn.

He has many hues, yet He is of one colour
He is the water and the wave
He is the temple and is the God therein
He is the priest, He is the prayer
He is the yogi, He is the Yoga.
The Lord of Nanak in all things you see
Yet the Lord is from all things free.

Mrit mandal jag sajiya

The world He created as a house of slaughter
Like castles of sand children make, it lasts not long
It rots as paper under the drip-drop of water.

See for yourself, in your mind weigh:
Yogis, men of action, and householders,
Have left their homes and belongings and gone their way.

As a dream at night, the world is such
And all you see must perish.
O Fool, why love you this world so much?

Open wide your eyes, see and learn:
Your friends and brothers in the shade are gone,
Some have left, others await their turn.
Only those who have served the Lord absolute
Find their places at Hari's gates
They stand firm (and will not be turned away).

Nanak is the servant of the Lord
O destroyer of Evil, protect him.

Prabh ji tun mere pran adhare

O Lord, You are the hope of my life,
You I greet, before You I prostrate myself
To You I offer salutations, to You I make sacrifice.

Seated or standing, in sleep or in waking
My thoughts ever turn to You.
My sorrows and joys, all that passes in my heart
I bring to You.

You are my support, my strength, my knowledge,
My wealth are You and all the kinsmen I have.
Says Nanak: What You do is for the best
He finds peace at the sight of Your feet.

MUNDAVAANI

Thaal vichi teeni vasute paiyo

On this platter you will find three things:
Truth, contentment and contemplation
Also the nectar of the name of the Lord
Which gives sustenance to life
He who imbibes and ingests it will be saved
No one can afford to give it up
Preserve it in your hearts forever and ever.
In the darkness spread over the world,
You will be saved by clasping the feet of the Lord
Says Nanak, for the whole expanse is the Lord's.

GURU
TEGH BAHADUR

{1621–1675}

In all, 115 hymns of the ninth Guru were
incorporated in the Adi Granth by his son and the last Guru,
Gobind Singh.

Birtha kahon kaun sion man ki

Whom shall I tell of the anguish of my heart?
Greed has me in its hold.
I rush madly in the ten directions
Seeking gold.
I suffer much wanting life of ease
And serve all kinds of people,
And like a dog go from door to door
But I have no thought of prayer.
I waste my human existence,
I have no shame when people laugh at me.
O Nanak, why sing you not in praise of the Lord
And rid your mind and body of impure thoughts?

Jo nar dukh mai dukh nahi manai

He who in adversity grieves not
He who is without fear
He who falls not in the snare of sensuality
Who has no greed for gold knowing it is like dust.
He who does not slander people when their backs are turned
Nor flatters them to their faces.
He who has neither gluttony in his heart
Nor vanity nor attachment with worldly things.
He whom nothing moves,
Neither good fortune nor ill,
Who cares not for the world's applause,
Nor its censure,
Who ignores every wishful fantasy
And accepts what comes his way as it comes.
He whom lust cannot lure
Nor anger command,
In such a one lives God Himself.
On such a man does the Guru's Grace descend,
For he knows the righteous path.
O Nanak, his soul mingles with the Lord
As water mingles with water.

Sadho eh tan mithiya jano

This body is a lie, O Seers,
The spirit of God within the only truth.
Why do you wallow in sweet illusions,
Why are you attached to worldly possessions

When nothing will go with thee?
Put away all thoughts of praise or blame,
And fix your mind on His glory.
In every heart dwells the Perfect One,
Says Nanak, know him as the Lord.

Sukh main bahu sangi bhaye

Many were my friends in the hour of happiness,
In sorrow none remains.
Says Nanak, recite the Lord's Name, O mind,
He alone is yours in the end.

Na hi gun na hi kachhu jap tap

I possess no virtue, nor merit of worship;
How shall I redeem myself?
Says Nanak, Thou art my only refuge,
Give me the boon of courage, O Lord.

Jagat bhikhari firat hai

All the world is a wandering beggar,
The Lord alone is the bestower.

Says Nanak, remember Him, O heart,
Then all your efforts bear fruit.

Bar bhiti banai rachi pachi

A wall raised of sand
Will not last four days;
So are the joys of maya:
Know this, O mind, and be free.

GURU
GOBIND SINGH
{1666–1708}

Guru Gobind Singh added his father's compositions in the
Adi Granth, but none of his own. His writings are collected
in the *Dasam Granth*. Many of the last Guru's hymns are
used in Sikh ritual and prayer, especially the
evening prayer, Rehras.

From *Akaal Ustat:*

As sparks flying out of a flame
Fall back on the fire from which they rise;
As dust rising from the earth
Falls back upon the same earth;
As waves beating upon the shingle
Recede, and in the ocean mingle
So from God come all things under the sun
And to God return when their race is done.

Mitter Piyare nun, haal mureedan da kehnan

Beloved Friend, beloved God, Thou must hear
Thy servant's plight: when Thou art not near
The comforts' cloak is a pall of pest,
The home is like a serpent's nest;
The wine chokes like a hangman's noose,

The rim of the goblet is an assassin's knife.
With Thee shall I in adversity dwell,
Without Thee life in ease is life in hell.

Ap hath dae mujhae ubariyae

With Your own hands uplift me
From fear of death set me free;
Forever remain on my side
May Your sabre and banner by me abide.

Rakhi lehu muhi rakhanhare

Protect me O Great Protector
Lord of saints, helper of your loved ones;
Always friend of the poor, foe of the evil remain
Lord, the fourteen worlds are within your domain.

Kal payi brahma bapu dhara

When the right time came You created Brahma the creator
When the right time came You created Shiva the destroyer
At the right time, You sent Vishnu the preserver;
Eternal time is Your plaything forever.

Javan kal sabh jagat banayo

He who did the entire world create
Also created gods, demons and yakshas;
He is the alpha and omega of time, the only incarnation
Understand that He is my only Guru.

Ghat ghat ke antar ki janat

The throbbing of every heart He hears
Pain of the good and wicked He knows;
From the tiny ant to the mighty elephant
He casts a benign look on all and is content.

Santan dukh paye te dukhi

When the godly suffer, He too suffers
When they are happy, He too rejoices;
The pain of those in pain He shares
The beating of every heart He hears.

Jab udakrakh kara kartara

In expansive mood the Creator did the world create
His creatures different shapes and forms did take;

Whenever He withdraws in Himself in a whim
All of them will merge in Him.

Nirankar Nribikar Nirlambh

Formless, immaculate, self-supporting
Primal, stainless, beyond time, self-born;
Only fools try to probe into His existence
Even sacred texts know not His essence.

Ekae rup anup sarupa

You are in many forms manifest
At one place You are a beggar, at another a king;
You create life from egg, womb and sweat
And from the earth many riches beget.

Kahun phul raja hae baetha

At some places You are a flower-bedecked king sitting on his throne
At others You are a hermit shrunken to the bone;
Your creation is a display of wonderment
You were before time, through the ages, self-existent.

Khadag ket mae tihari

In the battlefield Your protection I crave
Extend your hand and Your servant save;
In every place be my guide and helper
From wickedness and sorrow grant me shelter.

Panyi gahe jab te tumre

Ever since I clutched Your feet,
My eyes have not beheld another.
With Ram, Rahim, Puran and Koran, and others I did not bother.
Of Simritis, Shastras, Vedas and other texts I took no notice.
It is by virtue of Your banner and Your sword,
What I have written is not mine but Your sacred word.

Sagal duar kau chchadi kae

I passed by all doors before I stopped at Yours
Hold me in Your arms, and my honour save
Gobind will forever be Your slave.

Dehra maseet soi puja au namaaz oi

He is in the temple as He is in the mosque,
He is in the Hindu worship as He is in the Muslim prayer.
Gods and demons who guard the treasures
Of the God of riches, the musicians celestial,
The Hindus and the Muslims—they are all one.
They have each the habits of different homes,
But all men have the same eyes, the same body,
The same form compounded of the same four elements—
Earth, air, fire and water.
Thus the Abhekh of the Hindus and the Allah of Muslims are one,
The Quran and the Puran praise the same Lord.
They are all of one form,
The one Lord made them all.

Kon bheo mundia sanyasi

One man by shaving his head
Hopes to become a holy monk,
Another sets up as a yogi
Or some other kind of ascetic.
Some call themselves Hindus
Others call themselves Mussalmans . . .
And yet man is of one race all over the world;
God as Creator, and God as Good
God in His Bounty and God in His Mercy
Is all One God. Even in our errors
We must not separate God from God!
Worship the One God,

For all men the One Divine Teacher.
All men have the same Form.
All men have the same Soul.

Naam thaam na jaat roop na rekh

He has no name, no dwelling-place, no caste;
He is the Primal Being, Gracious and Benign,
Unborn, Ever Perfect, and Eternal.
He is of no nation and wears no distinguishing garb;
He has no outer likeness; He is free from Desire.
To the east or the west,
Look where you may,
He pervades and prevails
As love and affection.

From *Bicitra Natak*:

For though my thoughts were lost in prayer
At the feet of Almighty God,
I was ordained to establish a sect and lay down its rules.
But whosoever regards me as Lord
Shall be damned and destroyed.

I am—and of this let there be no doubt—
I am but the slave of God, as other men are,
A beholder of the wonders of creation.

From *Zafarnama*:

I am the destroyer of turbulent hillmen
Since they are idolaters and I am the breaker of idols.

From *Svaiye*:

Some worship stones and on their heads bear them,
Some the phallus strung in necklaces wear its emblem.
Some behold their god in the south, some to the west bow their head.
Some worship images, others busy praying to the dead.
The world is thus bound in false ritual
And God's secret is still unread.

From *Jap Sahib*:

God has no friends nor enemies.
He needs no hallelujahs nor cares about curses.
Being the first and timeless
How could He manifest Himself through these
Who are born and die?

From *Sabad Hazare*:

Let thine own house be the forest
Thy heart the anchorite.
Eat little, sleep little,
Learn to love, be merciful and forbear.
Be mild, be patient,
Have no lust, nor wrath,
Greed nor obstinacy.

From *Candi Cartir*:

O Lord, these boons of Thee I ask,
Let me never shun a righteous task,
Let me be fearless when I go into battle,
Give me faith that victory will be mine,
Give me power to sing Thy praise,
And when comes the time to end my life,
Let me fall in mighty strife.